Contents

What is soil?

Soil is something found in nature.

It is everywhere in the world around us.

Soil is made of small rocks.

Soil is made of dead plants.

Types of soil

Soil can be wet.

Soil can be dry.

Soil can be made of peat.

Peat is made of plants that rotted a long time ago.

Soil can be made of clay.

Clay is made of rocks and old plants.

Clay is very heavy soil.

Soil can be made of sand.

Sand is made of rocks and shells.
Sand is light soil.

How do plants use soil?

Soil helps plants grow.

Soil holds plants in the ground.

Plants get food from soil.

Plants get water from soil.

How do people use soil?

Soil is used to grow plants.

Soil can be used to make buildings.

Different types of soil

◀ clay

▲ peat

◀ sand

Picture glossary

 **nature** the world around us. Plants, animals, rocks, water, and soil are part of nature.

 **shell** a hard covering that grows on some animals

Index

Notes for parents and teachers

Before reading   Talk to the children about how plants grow in soil. Explain that soil can be light (sandy), heavy (clay), or dark (peat). If possible, dig a small hole in a patch of soil and encourage the children to note what they see. Is the soil wet or dry? Is it soft to touch? Can they see anything in the soil? (There may be worms, woodlice, centipedes, or weeds.) Explain that soil has food in it that minibeasts and plants feed on.

After reading

• Help the children to plant a seed such as a bean in soil in a narrow glass jar. Ask them what they think the seed will need in order to grow (water and light). Observe the roots as they extend down into the soil.

• Make a wormery. Cut the top and bottom off a plastic bottle and place it in a plant pot. Fill it with layers of soil and sand. Put six worms in the soil. Leave a piece of vegetable at the top. Cover the bottle with black cloth. After a few days, remove the cloth and observe what the worms have been doing.

• Say the rhyme: "Under a stone where the soil was firm / I found a wiggly, wiggly worm / 'Good morning,' I said, 'how are you today?' / But the wiggly worm just wriggled away."

24